Temple of the Sacred Light

Temple of the Sacred Light

WORDS OF DEVOTION

By Ra (Rachelle Vitnell)

Recognise

Temple of the Sacred Light
Words of Devotion
By Ra (Rachelle Vitnell)

Foreword:

Your world is a reflection of you and you come to know yourself through that reflection.

Our relationships, our friendships, our families, our career, our environment all show us who we are through the reflection they mirror back to us. Those reflections become the reference points of our identity. The confirmation of who we are.

If you were to be without those reference points, if they were to all go, would you know who you are?

Could you see yourself outside of those close up reflections?

We truly have no idea what our reference points of self are and how much we rely on them until they are gone. Only then do we experience the void of reflection, the moment where we no longer know ourselves. When all traces of who we were are gone as all of the old mirrors fall away.

This is the moment when the caterpillar begins to turn into a butterfly. When the deepest transformation is taking place. When you are truly changing.

In the middle of that transformation is a void, when you are no longer caterpillar and not yet a butterfly. When there is no reflection that you recognise and you no longer know how to see yourself.

This time is confusing and can be extremely painful. Where the grief of loss for the old identity flows through your heart and the fear of being no one can take over your mind.

The dreaded wasteland of the lost self can be all consuming. The fear of never seeing yourself again can feel so real.

This place where you are no longer who you were and not yet who you will be is a place that most people avoid. It takes a deep inner strength to go to this place and courage to sit in for as long as it takes.

At first you grab at anything, trying to hold onto a fragment of your old reflection out of the knowing that when you let it go, you will never see yourself again, not the you that you were, that you, that identity will no longer exist.

Eventually you surrender to faith, to a deep trust that there will be another you on the other side, a you that is more you than you have ever been, a you that is a more authentic, a closer to your essence you.

When the transformation is complete and you emerge as the butterfly, your reflection no longer only comes from people and things close up, you learnt to see yourself in all things.

The trees, the flowers, the animals, the sun, the moon, the sky, the stars, the ocean the waves all become your reference points of self.

You see your own love reflected in all things and your reference points of your identity become infinite.

When you are no longer the finite self, with a limited reflection but you become an infinite being, when you take your place amongst the stars.

These words of devotion, these messages of love and grace are my gift to those who find themselves in the dark night of the soul, the chrysalis of death, journeying towards the rebirth.

No matter where you find yourself in that journey, either at the beginning or right in the thick of it, know that you are loved, you are felt and you are held by the light of all that is, as you make your way back home to the truth.

Through the ashes, we rise. A baptism of fire, followed by the falling of the ashes. As each ash falls, it touches the ground in a new place, transformed through its fiery metamorphosis, changing the landscape of our life once again.

My journey of awakening has been just like that. The intensity of the fire, giving way to the peaceful clarity of the falling ash.

Some of the messages on these following pages are small and simple, some are longer and more complex but all of them came through my soul in moments that I needed to hear them. Some days to soothe my aching heart, others to celebrate and rejoice in the light of truth. Each word birthing through me and changing my relationship to life itself.

I share them now as an act of devotion to the Sacred Light of all that is.

With love, Ra.

~
There will come a day when you are ready to be guided.
On that day, you will have truly surrendered and handed yourself
over to the will of yourself as the one infinite Creator.
~

If you were to truly open your heart, the whole world would rush in.

All of the suffering, all of the joy and everything in between would become present in your heart.

That is what having your heart open truly is.

Not just with the nice stuff but with all of the horror of humanity as well.

To bear it all and still know divinity.

Sometimes, if it is to be so, your soul will break your heart and shatter your world to move you to where you need to go.

This is the fiery metamorphosis, the tearing apart of comfort and complacency, the sacred death initiating you into a deeper truth of yourself.

If you can come into full realisation of this, all circumstance is forgiven, all suffering comes to completion and the old self is fully surrendered.

This is the rebirth, the ushering in of your higher path and you become the Phoenix having alchemised your suffering into love.

I am my own witness

I am my own loving appreciation

I am my own compassionate heart

I am my own graceful mercy

I am my own sacred prayer

I am my own guiding light

I am my own eternal flame

I am

We must not turn away from the light, no matter how much darkness we see.

And we must not turn away from the darkness, no matter how much light we see.

To be truly unified in the power of mercy, we must let the whole world into us and be with the suffering and the grace.

You cannot truly be of this world if you are not open to all of it.

At first when you open to all of the darkness, it will crush you and shatter you. Let it break you open.

At first when you open to all of the light, it will illuminate and liberate you. Let it break you open.

Open your eyes, become aware of it all. Allow all of it to exist fully. Only then can you ever truly have any impact, only then can you ever truly be of service to others in the reality of their experience.

Hold the light, shine it on the darkness within and without so that it too becomes the light.

As within, so without.

As above, so below.

Joy arises through surrender not circumstance.

All emotions are expressions of love, from lower expressions such as hate to higher expressions such as joy; often spoken as the Bliss State.

Pure Joy comes through freedom and freedom comes through surrender which seems contrary to the mind.

If you want to be free, you cannot push away anything. Freedom is the embracing of all things, the allowing of all things to exist and the clutching at none of them.

The positive spirituality path is not a path of freedom. You cannot get free by chasing positivity. You will forever be fearful of things that inspire the lower expression emotions and so you will be forced to manipulate your experience of things rather than being able to simply be present with what is; fully surrendered and therefore in a state of joy.

If your concept of the Bliss State is attached to circumstance, to following only what makes you happy then you will end up suffering through the ebbs and flows of life or only living in the shallows, denying the existence of the depths. This is not transcending the Ego, the separate self, this is further imprisoning yourself within it. Chasing Joy through fear, controlling circumstances and manipulating outcomes in order to feel safe.

Surrender means complete acceptance, completely allowing something to be as it is.

You know that you are fully surrendered when you are no longer attached to getting only your preferences met. When you can accept fully what is, as deeply as you would accept what you would prefer, as you have the wisdom to know that each outcome is equally as valuable.

In this state of awareness, joy arises naturally and full embodiment of the bliss state is possible.

And then one day you stop looking outside and you realise that it is you, it has always been you that you have been looking for.

You are the one.

You are your own Soul Mate.

And one day you let it all go
The what was
The what wasn't
And the what you wanted it to be

You let go
Release your suffering
And liberate your heart
On that day, your soul will rejoice
For its time has come to guide you with grace

And though you may be tired from the fight to control and hold on to all that you just let go of, you will be at peace, content and softened by the initiation of surrender.

What you fear is an illusion

The existential crisis of the one who believes it is separate from oneness

All stories are fictions of the mind, set to divide, to prove its own lie,

that we are not one

Let go into your fear

Let yourself enter the cave inside

The place from which you run and hide

Let your fear annihilate you

Let the one who fears, die

For truth is impervious to death

and what is true will rise

out of the flames of your own demise

Love has the power to heal and transform anything that it comes into contact with.

Those who know, understand.

You cannot shine your light in the darkness if you refuse to acknowledge its presence.

Do the shadow work. You can't bypass it, it doesn't go away.

Our work is to go into the darkness and shine the light to transform it from within.

As within, so without.

You came here for this and you are powerful beyond your current awareness.

You have a role to play in this life.

You soul has been preparing you.

Your destiny is calling.

It's time to remember who you are and what your mission here is.

What is the Matrix?

You are the Matrix. It is the construct of consciousness that you experience yourself within.

Freedom is not escaping from the Matrix, freedom is being responsible for your own creation of it.

To see the Matrix you only need to look around outside of you to see the correspondence in the mirror.

You are the cause of everything that affects you in your life.

You are also the only one who can change it through the recognition of yourself as all of it.

That is why all great teachers and gurus speak of oneness, of unity, of the non-dualistic self.

To awaken, you must realise the truth. You must come to understand the Matrix as yourself. You must accept that you are every single person and part of the very Matrix that you experience yourself within.

Nothing outside of you is separate to you. Everyone you encounter is an aspect of you waking yourself up, reminding you of who you really are.

You must embrace all of your perceivable reality as yourself to truly understand unity.

You cannot be truly empowered when you are at the effect of your own causes without the awareness that you are them and they are you.

You are creating and experiencing your own reality, your own Matrix and then trying to escape it by seeking change outside of yourself as if you believe that you are living within a story that is being written about you not by you.

This beautiful life you are living is showing you who you are and what you are capable of becoming. You just need to learn how to see.

There is a very big difference between wanting something and choosing it.

Wanting is placid and pliant, it is the decision to wait whereas choice inspires dedication,
commitment and devotion.

It is a process of taking affirming action.

Wanting and choosing have very different energetic vibrational patterns.

When you want something, your potential is limited by the energetic characteristics of wanting.

When you choose something your potential is limitless through the energetic possibilities of choice.

We are all one, dreaming of many.

Everything you experience outside of self, is just the nonintegrated self.

Once the self becomes integrated, it fully realises itself as everything.

Inside and outside cease to exist as all is one, all is the self.

Everything is only what it is because it is mutually beneficial.

Spiritual Growth is not a process of learning rather it is a journey of re-mem-ber-ing.

You are a member of the whole, a part of it like a body part, yet you have created an illusion for yourself that you are cut off from the whole, that you are separate.

Most people when they start out on the spiritual path think that they need to connect themselves back in with the whole, further perpetuating their own illusion of separation. For you would only need to return to the whole if you were actually separated from it but you only seem separate in your own illusion.

When you re-member who you are, you let go of the illusion in your mind.

You realise that every time you consider another as something outside of you or different to you, you are creating an illusion of separation for yourself that you will have to wake up from in order to realise yourself as the whole.

When you are cut off from the whole by illusion the only way you can function in life is to be fully identified with your Ego. You can do all of the 'work' on yourself from that place and yet you will only ever be mimicking your greatest potential not actualising it as truth.

The Ego will create an illusion of light for you to be mesmerised by. A version of you that you can comfortably live as your greatest potential and yet it will be an illusion. A castle built on sand that cannot weather the great storms of suffering that come through the experience of reality as form and will require constant enhancing and upgrading to hold its position.

To truly live your greatest potential, you must let go of the illusion of separation and realize yourself as awake and autonomous enlightenment, creating from infinite potential.

No one is having the same experience as you because they are your experience.

The path of becoming somebody, will keep the true path of becoming nobody hidden from you, even if your path of becoming somebody is a spiritual one.

Wisdom claims no perspective but is curious about them all.

It may be real, as in the experience of reality you are having in this moment, but it may not be true.

Love is the only truth.

Everything other than love is but a distortion of the truth.

See it, see your current reality but come back to love within yourself and your reality will then align with the truth of love.

Your perspective is the effect, caused by your level of understanding.

To change your perspective, you have to expand your understanding.

The internal play of cause and effect.

Your divinity is in your humanity. Not in just being a human but in the benevolence of your human nature.

To know your divinity, you must come to know the fullness of yourself; and when you do, when you arrive at that knowing, the truth of you will bring your heart into the holy union of self actualisation and your highest potential fulfilled.

Intuition - Inner tuition

The experience of your higher self/ascended self, leaving messages in moments like breadcrumbs showing you the next step to take on your path so you can have the experience that will teach you what you came here to remember.

Your path in life is your curriculum, your inner knowing is your tuition.

The journey is less about becoming and more about unbecoming.

The only thing you have to do to become who you are is un-become who you are not.

To awaken you must cease to dream and the dreaming is life.

So, to awaken you must cease to dream the dream of life and why would you, when the dream is all there is and it is so beautiful.

For what wakes up, is only God.

We are so blessed by the people we have in our lives.

They reflect to us who we are.

Our self-awareness is born from the experiences with others. There is no greater gift than that.

No matter if we perceive the relationship as good or bad, they will always offer us the gift of self-illumination.

As human beings we crave certainty, we crave absolutes. We want to believe we are open minded and yet we also want to believe that what we believe is the truth.

Having certainty makes us feel safe, that things are in control. That we have things figured out to a point that we feel comfortable.

When everything is certain, there are no possibilities.

Growth, expansion, even manifestation require uncertainty. For our minds to be open to the point of doubt having not decided what something is or isn't.

Having the wisdom to live in doubt allows you to remain open to everything.

The mind may hear this and rebel. The fear of uncertainty is so great in most that they will carefully control as much of life as possible while creating the illusion for themselves that they are open to life.

Fear is our greatest hurdle to overcome on the path of life, our greatest adversary. We fight to overcome our fear by creating certainty, locking ourselves into an ongoing battle with shadows and limiting ourselves to only what we already know.

Surrender is the only way to defeat our fear. To surrender our certainty, to embrace uncertainty and to open to the infinite possibilities of life, is our ultimate liberation.

Letting go, surrendering attachment is the gateway to waking up.

In order to see beyond the veil we must give up our attachment to it.

Your identity, your character blocks your view of your true nature. You cannot know the truth unless you are willing to give up the temporary lie.

I am not me, you are not you, we are not us. You will only come to know the truth of what this really means when you are ready. You have to awaken within your dream before you can awaken from your dream.

The path to yourself is not the path of striving and expanding outwardly, it is the path of unbecoming and collapsing inwardly.

There will come a point where you will cease to be you.

When the you that you know will pass over and will never be again.

While your soul or your higher self is eternal and will go on, the curtain will come down on this character and you will experience the finale of this self that you are now.

When this truth is accepted fully, the only response is love. Absolute recognition of the deep and unwavering love that you have for yourself.

And the thought of not savouring every moment of the time you get with yourself because of trivial self judgement seems so devastatingly sad in the face of this knowing.

When you awaken to the consciousness within you, you do not overcome the illusion of being human, you recognise the truth of being divine.

The presence of a villain is the invitation for a hero.

Allow whatever shows up in your world to call forward the hero in you.

And what is truly heroic is to awakening to your highest level of consciousness and act from there.

We are being called forward, we are being asked to rise. We are being beckoned to awaken to our true nature. To become the hero in our own life.

The old paradigm of rise and fight is not the answer anymore. We must rise in awareness and consciousness.

We must become warriors of the light.

We must confront ourselves and overcome the villain inside who judges and condemns and keeps us locked in fear.

We must become heroic in our pursuit of truth and love and the wisdom required to release ourselves from our own prisons.

To what have we enslaved ourselves?

Are we truly willing to be free?

Are we ready for what it really means to work together as one world in unity?

To become free, we must first become heroic.

Surrender with an agenda for what you want to come from that act of surrender is not surrender at all.

It is in fact, attachment through resistance and another form of manipulation and it is just the Ego bargaining through spiritual principles.

Enlightenment is not the end point but a whole new beginning.

It is to be illuminated by the light of your own being.

Earth is a school, we each have our own unique curriculum.

We just have to do our work, the work that is right in front of us as that is our path of initiation into higher dimensions of awareness.

Take a moment to feel into your heart, feel the truth and you will find the peace in the external chaos. Everything is ok, even if it seems like it is not.

You are safe, your soul is eternal, you are already wise beyond your own knowing.

Breathe, let go, trust your life, find faith, you are perfectly on track, finding your own way home to love.

I love you. I am here with you. You are seen. You are valued. You are safe in the light of grace.

Spirituality is not a vehicle to take you somewhere better than where you are now.

It is a pathway to becoming more compassionate, more whole.

United we thrive, divided we suffer.

Both within ourselves and in life with others.

As within, so without.

Love is your truth.

Anything that you are feeling that is other than love, is a distortion of the truth.

Notice it, pay attention to your feelings that take you away from the experience of love.

That is where your work is.

True love arises naturally within us as we open ourselves in acceptance of its constant presence.

Others cannot give us love, their presence can only invite us to become aware of the field of love that we are already a part of, the quantum field of consciousness that we are.

We continually settle for less than our true desires if we do not have faith in them arriving.

Faith gives us the wisdom and patience to surrender to the divine timing of things. To trust in what we want so deeply that we can let go and allow it to arrive in the perfect timing and perfect scenario.

If you have to keep hustling and pushing to make things happen, perhaps you have a faith issue.

If you believe completely in your dreams, the journey becomes more and more effortless. Synchronicities line up as you start to manipulate the energy field to allow your desire to manifest itself in your awareness.

This is where you start to learn the secrets of alchemy and wondrous things begin to open up before you.

Inspiration arises out of nowhere and says 'Do this Now' whereas Agenda induces action and is always creating plans out of options.

Agenda acts to avoid something we fear, Inspiration asks as to move beyond our fears.

So, if you wish to align yourself with Divine Inspiration, you must cultivate the patience to wait until it arrives and the courage to follow its lead once does.

Love is the only thing that heals and liberated us.

Any work we do on ourselves is simply the acknowledging and relinquishing of anything blocking our experience of love.

It is so very simple, it is just not easy.

We must to come out of the illusion that life is happening to us.

We must realise that whatever happens on our path is put there by our higher self as it offers the greatest opportunity for our evolution.

We are initiating ourselves into higher levels of consciousness through our life experiences.

So often we are trying to love ourselves without accepting all of the different aspects that make us who we are.

Our identity is layered and complex. It is dualistic in nature, made up of shadow and light.

You cannot hate or shame yourself into changing and you cannot love what you don't accept.

So you see, acceptance is the key to self love that transforms and transcends your inner duality.

And so today, just live.

Have faith in all that you are, you are already your highest potential in every moment.

Have trust in your path, that it is unfolding exactly as it's meant to.

Now is all there is, so be here now in perfect love and perfect trust.

You are held, you are safe, you are seen and valued by the light of all that is.

So today, go and live.

A radical shift has taken place.

A great change has already occurred.

What happens from here will be very important.

You are being called into your highest potential.

You are being asked to find faith and leap into the unknown.

You are more ready than you realize.

You ARE what you came here to DO.

So go do you and the path will appear as you walk on it.

Breathe, trust, surrender, then move.

Just be yourself. Nothing more is needed and nothing less will do.

You can liberate yourself from you past hurts and trauma if you are willing to do the inner work to heal, forgive, let go and transcend your current level of awareness.

In the higher realms of awareness, there are no victims. Everything that happens is an initiation into higher levels if your potential. A beneficial experience for the awakening consciousness.

When life is understood from a higher order of things, the experience of life changes and you become liberated from the past and the future, to exist only in the here and the now.

That is true sovereignty.

Codependency is the process of needing others to fulfil the emotional needs that we are not meeting within ourselves.

And as we are unable to receive from others that which we are not already in relationship with in ourselves, we set the people around us up with an impossible task.

It is the child within us refusing our own love and trying to get it from Mum & Dad still, through our primary relationships, family, friends, colleagues etc.

This unconscious dynamic is at the root of all conflict and emotional suffering.

The conscious path is one of self-responsibility, taking the necessary steps to identify and meet our own needs, so that we are able to receive unconditionally from those around us.

When our needs are met, we are free to enjoy what is offered to us through our relationships and we are also free to move away if what is offered is not in alignment for us.

It is up to us to ensure that our needs are met, that we feel safe within ourselves so that we may show up in the world free and liberated. So that we can enjoy our relationships with others and all that they add to our experience of life from a conscious and emotionally stable place.

Self-responsibility is the spiritual journey and it is the pathway of Self Mastery.

Connection is at the heart of the experience of reality.

We come to know ourselves through interacting with our environment, with others, especially when the interaction is consistent as in friendships/relationships.

The power is in taking responsibility for our own self-awareness through the experience of our connections so that we may come to know deeper and deeper truths of ourselves.

Life is a reflection, it takes practice to learn how to understand what we see.

Harmony

To be in acceptance of what is, working with the energy.

Harnessing the available flow.

Riding the current of life.

Gracefully gliding on the wind, allowing it to take you where you are going.

Being at peace inside so that there is no friction outside.

Experiencing the Zen, within the chaos.

Recognising what is needed and sincerely being of service to that.

Being love.

Life is a grand adventure.

Duality is an exquisitely painful companion.

Openness to it all is the only requirement to live it with grace.

Becoming the observer of your life, witnessing yourself as you would a child, watching yourself move through life learning and growing is endearing to the point that you cannot continue to avoid loving yourself.

Becoming the conscious observer is an evolutionary step towards spiritual mastery and loving yourself means opening yourself to love.

Love is always there waiting for you to become aware of it, as you master the art of opening.

The only way to transform your current reality is to transcend the distortions of truth within you that created it.

There is nothing happening outside of you that is not a projection of your mind/mentality.

All is Mental, All is mind.

If you understand that you are creating this, then you can discover why you are creating it. Everything is always for your highest evolutionary benefit.

You can use your current experience of reality to transcend yourself. You can use the external phenomena of circumstance to be your catapult into your highest potential.

All growth, all healing is simply this.

You are already doing it, often you are just not aware of the deeper aspects of what is really occurring.

If you don't understand, be curious, seek understanding. It is your pathway to liberation and only you can take yourself there.

We accumulate layers and layers of density, of distortions of truth that cover over the purity of who we are through belief and programming. Like putting on layers of clothing that hide our true selves, until we reach a turning point in our evolution.

A catalytic moment that changes the trajectory of our focus from outward expansion to inward revelation.

This change in perceptional direction begins a journey of unraveling all of the weaving of personal and societal concepts we have created as our fabric of reality.

We go from creating our identity through an external feedback loop to unveiling our true nature to ourselves.

This peeling back process is the spiritual journey, a conscious undoing to become what always was.

The closer you get to the core, the thinner the layers are like translucent membranes barely perceptible yet still very much clouding the truth.

There seems to be a moment when you get deep enough, when you are so close to the purity that the realisation of the push and pull within ourselves becomes apparent. Where we realise that we both want to unveil our true self and yet we are afraid of letting go of the layers that we have lived through for so long. The realisation that to let go is to let die the person you have been, the one that you think you are. The ego death that we chase is also what we fear the most as it is the ultimate and permanent ending of our own illusion.

Consciousness is always streaming through us, pulling us forward to the next moment, along the continuum of expansion.

Seemingly unrelated moments only reveal their secret synergistic nature when our expansion reaches a certain vantage point of recognition.

Cause and effect are always at play, weaving the tapestry of our reality.

You are God, creating a universe through thought.

The journey is to fall in love with love itself.

Once you exist in that space, you no longer need another to inspire love in you and you will be truly free to have unconditionally loving relationships as you will choose the person who compliments your authenticity the most.

Our relationships are reflections of ourselves.

If you are not in full acceptance of yourself, you will pull in relationships that will show you where you are out of alignment, the parts of yourself that you need to awaken through love.

We seek to master our karmic lessons through the polarity of duality with others.

The sacred and loving act of releasing ourselves through the experience of each other.

There is no more higher purpose in this life than this. This is the deeper understand of the mirror.

And when it is done, when we finally come to the moment of release, within one moment we will come to know the perfection of it all and it is truly beautiful. We sit in the stillness of singularity, all being one, all being grace.

The Universe will evict you from your inauthentic life if you don't get the message and leave.

So often we are trying to love ourselves without accepting all of the different aspects that make us who we are.

Our identity is layered and complex. It is dualistic in nature, made up of shadow and light.

You cannot hate or shame yourself into changing and you cannot love what you don't accept.

So you see, acceptance is the key to self love that transforms and transcends your inner polarisation.

We block our own needs from being met with the belief that we are somehow unworthy of them and then project that experience onto our partner, family, friends or even life itself.

This is the real battle, the internal push and pull, the game that we play inside ourselves that creates our suffering and disappointment as we try to win the game through others in distorted and messy patterns of unconscious codependency.

We are unaware that we are making everyone else responsible for us, demanding that they show up in the right way and meet our needs to try and overcome our own self appointed beliefs of not being worthy of them, all through unconscious patterns of behaviour. We demand that they meet this impossible task and if they don't we blame them, we call them selfish, narcissistic, accuse them of not caring about us.

As we shift internally, the external world shifts and changes to reflect that. As we become aware of our own needs and choose to be responsible for fulfilling them, be it by ourselves or if necessary asking for that need to be met by another, we change our internal game and break the codependency cycles. Our connection with others starts to become more simple, we feel more met, more loved, more at ease in the world. We start to see our part in the distortions of relating, we can see clearly our role in the messes we have experienced in life.

This is growth, this is sovereignty. It takes work, it takes courage and it takes humility to stop blaming others for every bit of suffering and dissatisfaction we experience long enough for us to see the internal game that is setting it all up.

Belief equals reality.

But Beliefs can be changed, not matter how long they have been held or how crystallised they may seem.

Therefore, reality is changeable.

You are always in control of what you experience.

No matter how removed you are right now from the creation of your reality, you can at any point stop to examine your beliefs and therefore become consciously engaged in the what you are choosing to experience.

Write about what you don't want, what you do want, write about it all.

Express it, share it out into the world.

Cast a spell with your words.

Cast it outwards, spread the ashes, sow the seeds and so mote it be.

In order to transcend the reality of dark and light, you need to recognise that you are made up of both.

There is no dark and light outside of you, you have created them both and are created by both.

Our purpose is not to strive for one or the other but to acknowledge the purpose of both and find the balance of harmony at the Centre.

Ecstatic bliss is the experience of balance not the clutching at joy alone.

The only thing that stops us from being fully awakened, is that thought that we are not.

So, you see, the very idea that we have to overcome anything is the very thing that keeps you trapped by it.

If you want to be free, give up your thoughts.

Align with soul truth, consciousness, the All and you will open to the magic of manifestation.

Anything other than that is not manifestation just a manipulation of the Ego, trying to affect and assert control over the situation and the outcome based on the agenda that is always self (Ego) serving.

The truth is, you are either in Ego or out of it. Coming from the infinite self or the limited perception.

I searched in books and texts

I searched in people and places

I searched in workshops and retreats

I searched up mountains and in creeks

I searched everywhere for me

My search took me far, it took me wide

It took me here and there

It took me into pain and pleasure, suffering and emptiness

But the only place I found myself, was in the spaces in between

Love is a matter of acceptance. A space in which both the highest vision and the present moment are held simultaneously and yet one does not diminish or concede to the other.

Love is perceiving the divinity and humanity all at once and embracing both with pure, devout acknowledgement of the breathtaking truth of that union.

Love is allowing the passage of time to give birth to wisdom, having faith that it will.

Love is the patience to hold space without attachment and the courage that it takes to do so.

Love is the truth behind all illusion. It is the essence that holds us, the source of all that is.

Love is.

The Apocalypse, the end of life as we know it is a much feared idea from theology, that has filtered through many realms of society.

However, the word itself in Greek means 'to lift the veil'. Lifting the veil is too illuminate, too enlighten to truth, as once the veil is lifted, that which was not able to be perceived before becomes available. And then, all is revealed.

A situation becomes multifaceted once you learn to perceive beyond your own individual experience.

So the concept of the Apocalypse may just be more of a metaphor to teach than a literal warning of impending doom.

Perhaps the message is that of a coming ending to one perception and awakening to another, one that is more connected, more inclusive and less rooted in the 'I' experience of life lived through the Ego.

Perhaps the Apocalypse is not the end of all life, but the end of life as it has been. An awakening into enlightenment that will mark the death of the ego and awakening of the soul both individually and collectively.

The universe is impartial because it is infinite.

In order to be infinite, ALL possibilities have to be available; good and bad in perfect balance.

If we want benevolence, that is up to us.

To think with benevolence towards ourselves and others.

To act with benevolence towards ourselves and others.

Letting go doesn't just take time, it takes presence.

The Art of Dissolution.

Each moment is a chrysalis for an infinitely expanding transformation

Each season, a preparatory state for the next

Each new awareness, a changing iteration of self

We are ceaselessly unfolding, mercilessly surrendering that which no longer is

Each breath out, the last

Each breath in, the first

Death and rebirth, the very flow that carries us through life

Dissolution at the core of our very nature

Impermanence the only permanent truth

Let yourself go

Surrender

Be done

Over and over and over and over again

Give yourself over to life, to love, to divinity, to grace itself, for you are the created and your only purpose it to be that which you already are.

Life will destroy and dismantle only who you no longer are.

Choosing yourself means more than just not allowing someone to treat you badly. It is also choosing to not treat yourself badly by allowing others to do so.

Choosing yourself also means accepting yourself fully. Not trying to change yourself so that you can be better but recognising your beauty and worth just as you are.

Choosing yourself is choosing to go after what is in your heart, no matter what.

It is loving, accepting and validating who you are so much that you don't need it from anyone else.

It is letting go of all of the ways you are trying to be somebody and just being who you are.

It is opening yourself fully to yourself in the deepest most honest level of intimacy.

Choosing yourself means acknowledging and honouring whatever is true for you and living your life accordingly.

Choosing yourself is taking responsibility for your own needs, emotion, physical, mental and spiritual and making sure that you honour them in the most gracious and loving way that you can.

Choosing yourself is an act of devotion, of commitment, of inner authority and sovereignty.

It is feeling the calling in your soul, the divine inspiration pulling you towards your destiny and taking the leap of faith without any safety net or mental security blanket.

There is no half doing it.

You can't choose yourself a little bit.

Choosing yourself is going all in, it is the biggest commitment you will ever make.

Wherever you are on the pathway towards choosing yourself fully, keep going. You have to keep choosing to let go of who you are not until you are ready to choose to be who you really are.

Pain taught me to see the world through the eyes of love.

Everyone has pain, everyone suffers.

My pain brought me closer to people, that is compassion.

When we break open so completely that we become fully connected to everything.

When we see the light shining through the cracks of our own suffering.

When we let go and give ourselves fully to our grief.

That is when we see it, the Collateral Beauty that comes after the surrender.

I pray that you let go and surrender, that you let yourself leap without plan or strategy so that you may discover what is always there waiting to catch you.

I pray that you relinquish your silent fight for control so that you may open with faith to all that is there guiding you, if only you are able to stop looking and start to see.

I pray that you feel safe enough to walk through your life with your heart wide open, knowing no borders or edges of your capacity to love.

I pray that when sadness visits you that you recognise it as an old friend and invite it in, knowing that the visit will bring so much more depth and richness to your life.

I pray that pain teaches you of your strength and shows you the resilience of your spirit and you learn to trust your capacity to survive.

I pray that failure brings to you humility and the gift of having to find the courage to try again.

I pray that redemption finds its way into your heart, as you learn to forgive and surrender your pain back into love.

I pray that you find Grace in the everydayness of life and are soothed by the magnitude of its wisdom.

I pray that you devote yourself to being an anchor for the light, illumination the shadow so that it too can be loved.

I pray that right now in this moment, you have peace in your heart knowing the perfection of all that is.

Choose to love unconditionally and choose to work towards releasing all judgements and expectations that keep you from that.

Choose to take on the courageous task of opening your heart to the whole world, just as it is.

Choose to learn the art if separating the soul from the incarnation. Not to condone hurtful or horrendous behaviour but also not to shut out of your heart those that engage in it.

To love beyond action and deed, to love in-spite of suffering and pain, to love without apology or explanation, just to love the truth of who we all are beyond what we see with only our eyes.

Love is the strongest force there is, love is oneness. Love is the singularity beyond separation.

Love is our true essence, our source, our home.

Love is Christ Consciousness, love is what this world needs more of, love is our true saviour, love is redemption.

To acknowledge the divine orchestration of all that is, is to love unconditionally and to love unconditionally is to bring about awakening.

I hope that your words change over time. That the space in which you speak from evolves.

I hope that you read your own words or hear yourself speak and recognise your contradictions from your last communication.

I hope you notice your position on things changing, your view points shifting as you do the work to view things from as many sides as you can.

I hope you look back over time of the things that you have shared and notice your evolution through not just your simplification of explanation but also your softening.

For if what you said a year ago or even just a month ago is exactly the same as what you are saying now, without any obvious shift or expansion, then you have not grown and you have not shifted and you certainly have not become more aware.

Awakening is self-evident, yet not always understood.

The most empowering thing that you can do for yourself is to courageously choose to be exactly where you are at.

To surrender any judgment of the circumstances that you find yourself in, to surrender any desire to be anywhere else and simply yet enthusiastically choose to be exactly where you are at.

To acknowledge a higher wisdom beyond yourself and to recognize that while you may not have chosen the moment you are in, that you were chosen for this moment.

To settle into each experience with the knowing that all is divinely ordered and orchestrated and all that is required of you is your full participation in the experience that you find yourself in.

To let go of the idea that you should be somewhere else and choose to be where you are at, relaxing into the embrace of the divine.

You are safe, you are held, you are loved beyond your minds capacity to comprehend and you are exactly where you have been chosen to be, so all you have to do is choose to be there.

What would happen if you were to there's nothing to forgive anyone for?

When you travel through forgiveness, then beyond it, you will come to know the truth of life. Then the true work begins. The work to bring all parts of you into remembrance of that truth, back home to grace.

I used to love so fiercely

For my love was so insecure that it needed protection

Now I love so gently

As my love is so self-assured that is knows no fear

There is nothing to be done with our suffering, except to feel it.

To surrender to it. To be with it. To give it our full presence.

Destiny is a funny thing.

It shows you your path and then waits for you to choose it.

Everyone is experiencing their own version of reality.

Every version is different from the others, even if it is only slightly varied.

Every version is absolutely true and correct.

Every version represents an entire universe unto itself.

Every version is valid and necessary.

Every version is a part of and has parts of the whole.

Every version is a focal point of consciousness, oneness experiencing all there is to experience through the collective illusion of separateness.

There is no one version that is more true, more correct, more valid, more right, more aware are more awakened. That is a fallacy of the Ego, an attempt at divinity without the acceptance of all that is divine.

There is no higher or lower. There is no truth and there is no lie.

Judgment is but an instrument of the Ego to attempt distill the infinite down to a controllable finite. All attempts at this are futile. You can close your eyes to the world but the world does not go away just because you do. Just as you can shut yourself off to the infinite and yet it remains infinite regardless.

The only answer to any possible question is acceptance. All is pure, all is divine, all is one.

Rise above your suffering, deepen beyond your hate and come home to your true nature, leaving the door of compassion open and the light of love on for those who are yet to find their way.

To become who you are meant to be, you have to be completely done with being who you currently are.

Don't choose what is easy, choose what is true.

Your heart will know what you want, don't let your head talk you out of it.

Knowing what your heart wants is only the beginning. Then you have to find the conviction to follow it, completely.

When you have your potential tied up with our self worth, you will limit yourself by how you see yourself not by and true limitation.

You unlock your full potential by truly accepting yourself, just as you are.

Strive to empty yourself so much that you make space for each moment to envelope you with its full embodied presence.

Consciousness is light, pure information.

The more you expand your capacity to open to pure consciousness, the more light/information is available to you.

We are here to know and master all things, through as many lifetimes as that takes.

We cannot learn what we do not experience and we will not transcend what we cannot master and until we surrender to that truth, we will continue to suffer.

We seek to master our karmic lessons through the polarity of duality with others.

The sacred and loving act of releasing ourselves through the experience of each other.

There is no more higher purpose in this life than this.

This is the deeper understand of the mirror.

And when it is done, when we finally come to the moment of release, within one moment we will come to know the perfection of it all and it will be beautiful. We will sit in the stillness of singularity, all being one, all being grace.

I'm sorry, please forgive me, thank you, I love you.

Thought is real, physical is the illusion.

What is true in our minds is true, even if others don't know it.

The Ego self, the identity, is the point of awareness on the wave of consciousness.

We are but a focal point for The All.

There is only The Self and The All, forever merging and emerging, through life and death. The dreaming and the awakening in a never ending fractal of infinite iterations.

We are not here to make sense of our lives.

The very idea that it must make sense is polarised in judgement.

It is decisive and it separates us from ourselves.

Searching for meaningful lessons is akin to a safety blanket, a pacifying comforter.

There is nothing wrong with whatever is.

The idea that there is comes from the Ego, posing as consciousness.

When you dream at night, you do not blame your dreaming self for not knowing it is a dream because you know that to your dreaming self it is not a dream, it is reality.

So, you should not blame yourself for not awakening while you are in this reality, because to yourself this dream is your reality.

We are not here to awaken, awakening is an illusion for we are not truly asleep. Awakening is dreaming us, purposefully, deliberately and wholeheartedly. The dream is our existence, we do not exist outside of our dream.

WE, as in the 'I' (I is for identity) cannot awaken. Awakening comes when it is time to surrender the 'I' and leave this dreaming behind, awakening birthing us into a new dream.

Embrace your dreaming, it is all that YOU have and it is beautiful.

The purpose of life is to become consciously aware of self. That is why we are endowed with the gift of consciousness.

The universe is fractal in nature, unending repeating patterns on a smaller and smaller scale.

From the infinite collective consciousness down to the individual, the purpose is the same, expansion.

Nothing more is needed and nothing less will do.

Life is a series of inhales and exhales.

The inhale is the healing, the rest, the slowing down, the being, the integration, the self-reflection, the creation. It is the inner journey.

The exhale is the movement, the momentum, the future pull, the living of wisdom, the action, the manifestation. It is the outer expression.

The longer we allow the inhale to be, the more powerful the exhale will be.

Consciousness is light, pure information.

The more you expand your capacity to open to pure consciousness, the more light/information is available to you.

Everything you witness in those around you is simply a reflection of yourself.

What you judge and make wrong in others, what you admire and celebrate in others.

If you cannot see where you are the same as what you are observing, then you cannot see yourself.

When you have your potential tied up with our self worth, you will limit yourself by how you see yourself not by and true limitation.

You unlock your full potential by truly accepting yourself, just as you are.

What is the pain that you are avoiding?

That deep cavern of churning that you have covered over with so many layers and

buried so deep for so long that you have almost forgotten it's there.

The searing affront of torment, that burns inside and forges a fire that torches the light of your heart.

It ravages you from the inside, scaring and robbing your heart of its suppleness.

Trauma takes with it any warmth, any safety and ease and replaces it with cold hearted fear of life and love itself.

A barren landscape where love and betrayal become synonymous and trust is impossible without armour.

The game of survival juxtaposed with the desperate search for love and connection and yet seen as the very same thing.

What is the pain you have buried? Can you even remember?

Is it so far away that you only feel it as if an echo, the faint awareness of something left behind?

Can you touch it or does it elude you even as it throbs its way through your nervous system;

haunting you from inside?

The cave you fear to enter, the terror you run from, the darkness in your heart the renders you paralysed.

The quacking tremor in your bones turning itself into shadow and permeating the very foundation of you.

The core, the place of conception of fear and the creation of swords and mirrors and sharp tongues.

What is the pain that you fear?

The pain the needs to be felt, baptising you into the throws of suffering where every moment, every memory, every feeling must flood you and consume you to the point of death, the point of surrender, so that you may be reborn by the virtue grace itself.

Life moves on in little ways every day

From death to rebirth as we ache and we pray

Life ebbs and flows through words and pros

And hearts do mend that once were broke

A smile, a laugh, a tear, a cry

The moments between moments when the sun does shine

A longing, a reaching, a beckoning forth

Life carries us along its meandering course

No matter how bleak, no matter how dark

Life finds a way to renew its spark

You will never know where the path may lead if you do not find the faith to follow it.

Strive to empty yourself so much that you make space for each moment to envelope you with its full embodied presence.

Losing someone you love, becomes an invitation to love ourselves more.

The very loss of that person allows the parts of ourselves that we were relying on the energy and presence of that person to fulfil to ache so much they become aware to us.

It illuminates the parts of us that have not been integrated and that are blocking our true sovereignty.

Loss is a master teacher when we know how to learn from it.

If you run from your pain

You run from your body

If you run from your body

You run from healing

If you run from your healing

You run from your humanness

If you run from your humanness

You run from your joy

If you run from your joy

You run from your divinity

Our Spiritual Path is through our humanness, through the mind, body connection and facilitated by the pain and the joy of the heart.

All that is real is love.

When all of the illusions of perception born of wound and belief are gone, the only thing that remains is love.

Love is our truth.

The underlying state of being, constantly present and yet covered over by layers of fear and survival.

Our only work is to discover and remove those layers. To deliver ourselves from fear and return ourselves to our truth, to love.

That is the Alchemy of the Soul.

Love is the state of surrendered acceptance.

The more you delve into spiritualism, the more truth you uncover for yourself, the more you will come to regard your humanness with the utmost respect and reverence.

To really get that the entire purpose of this life is to be human, to live within our humanity and at the same time evolve it through conscious spiritual awareness and practice is the very purpose of our existence is like coming full circle.

To be present with the spiral of awakening.

There is no real option of bypassing anything. When people think they are bypassing, they are in fact stalling their awakening. Prolonging the suffering of the dualistic experience that they are trying to avoid.

The human is the hero in our story. The opening of our heart and third eye to embrace our spiritual essence and integrate that into our humanness is the ultimate destination of our journey.

We will never reach our intended destination if we fail to recognise the significance of our humanness, embrace it fully and wake up from our own self-created delusions of spiritual grandeur. If we cannot in fact be authentic and real and raw.

Over identification with our 'spiritual self' is just another way of trying to overcome our negative beliefs of self. That without this level of spiritual significance, we are in fact not enough. It is just another game, a self-fulfilling prophecy created by our focused attention on our 'not enoughness' that continues to give power to that very belief by our engagement and participation with it.

Awakening = Embodiment, delivering ourselves into complete presence and awareness within all that we are, moment by moment.

Face it dear one, face it. Find the courage to turn around and face that truth that you are running from. You know what it is, you know the truth, turn around, just turn around.

Let the truth rush through your heart and break it open and as it heals, you will be set free.

We both exist in a universe and are a youniverse, all at the same time.

Everything is a fractal of a fractal. The unfolding of infinity.

Awakening is like a puzzle. We get it in pieces.

The more pieces we put together the more we can see of the bigger picture. It's the same for all of us but the speed of which we put the puzzle together throughout our lives varies. Some pieces take years to place while others take seconds.

Love is a matter of acceptance. A space in which both the highest vision and the present moment are held simultaneously and yet one does not diminish or concede to the other.

Love is perceiving the divinity and humanity all at once and embracing both with pure, devout acknowledgement of the breathtaking truth of that union.

Love is allowing the passage of time to give birth to wisdom, having faith that it will.

Love is the patience to hold space without attachment and the courage that it takes to do so.

Love is letting ourselves & others voluntarily evolve.

Self-awareness is not a fixed state. We do not arrive at being self-aware one time and stay that way forever. If we fail to continue to examine our thoughts, words and actions we very quickly loose our self-awareness, we become aware of who we were, not who we are.

Check in with yourself regularly. Qualify yourself. Qualify your thoughts, actions, reactions, ask yourself 'Is this the truth or is it a lie?' 'Am I being completely honest or am I compromising myself for an outcome?'

Self-awareness is a continual practice of self-examination and radical candor. Allowing ourselves to acknowledge the truth of where we are at in any point in time and being courageous enough to not minimise ourselves or lie to ourselves is what it takes.

We don't make mistakes, we make choices. If we look back and examine those choices, we will see our current level of awareness at the time that we made them.

Our hearts are pure and innocent, the suffering that we create for ourselves is only due to our incapacity to open to love. When you examine our past choices, see who we have been through this understanding we get to see where we need to grow. We get to come into relationship with all of ourselves and learn the lessons we came here to learn.

We learn through pain until we grow enough to learn through joy.

We are so free that we can choose bondage but we are not free from the consequences of our choices.

Free Will allows you to see yourself however you choose to, but however you see yourself becomes the reality that you live. Learn to observe your reality and you will find yourself there reflected back in the circumstances that you experience.

Witness the exquisite complexity of yourself through the reality you are living. Everything you see, hear, feel and experience is all you, the tapestry of reality that you have woven for yourself.

Be in awe of the miracle of this experience. The deep and profound understanding that you are the creator and the created, the painter and the painting, conductor and the symphony.

Do you know the difference between the two? For they are not the same and yet they are one.

The Divine Will of the master plan and the Free Will on the journey through it.

No true Kingdom/Queendom was ever built by a heart too fearful to be pure.

Are you prepared to lose yourself?

It's the only real way to find who you are.

The longer we spend participating in the idea of who we are the more that idea grows into a reality that defines us.

The definition of who we are can get in the way of us becoming who we are meant to be.

Authenticity is something we grow in to by unbecoming who we are 'being'.

It's only when we stop trying to be who we are and just simply be, that we can truly know who we are.

We have to let go in order to truly show up.

Surrendering the attachment to overcoming our limited self-belief is key to getting out of the story, the loop of feeling less so trying everything to become more.

When we let go, we flow in a state of acceptance, surrendering attachment and therefor no longer participating in the Ego Story.

Our Authentic Self lies beyond the reach of our Ego. Let go, find the courage to surrender the need for control, for it is only an illusion anyway, and open to the magic of what lies beneath.

It is only the Ego that believes it can create a life that is better than the one being laid out by the divine.

There comes a time for the story to end. For that which has been playing out to fade away and the wisdom gained to propel you into the next journey ahead.

Let things end, let doors close, allow the universe to guide you for it speaks to your soul.

There is a purpose for your life beyond the comprehension of your Ego. To align with it, all you have to do is sit with yourself long enough until you finally surrender the illusion of control and have faith enough to let things be as they are.

As we rebirth the light flows through the cracks in our Ego's armour, through the masks it wears as its identity.

This light, is the light of truth, illuminating and revealing our true nature, our true beauty.

The masks can deceive us into thinking they are true beauty but they are just constructs of all of the other masks that we have seen and been taught are beautiful.

Awakening allows the light, the true beauty of love to flow out and illuminate the essence from within in divine rapture and grace. Only then can we truly experience and appreciate how beautiful we truly are.

Acceptance of what is, even when it is not what we want requires faith and trust that every moment in our life is purposeful. That any pain or loss comes with a gold seam hidden in the silver lining that once understood will help is to find a deeper sense of joy and love.

Relationships end, friendships fade, life as we know it can alter right before our eyes. The cycle of birth, death and rebirth is lived throughout our life journey, over and over again. People, places and things will come and go.

As we journey through our life, evolving through our story, the scenery will change, the players will change, some will decide to exit your story and others you will leave behind. We are tasked to master acceptance as a part of our awakening, as a conduit for the calling in of our very evolution.

Acceptance is the keeper of the present moment, ushering us into the now, to the only moment that truly exists. It delivers us from the torment of the replaying of what has been and from the worry and fear of what may be. For neither the past or the future actually exist other than in the mind and all we have is now.

When we are fully present we are open to and connect with ALL that is, everything that could be is available to us and acceptance is the gateway to this magic of possibilities.

Love, the journey of our heart. The Master Teacher of the art of non-judgment, essential to transcending the EGO Identity.

Unconditional love is our true nature, it is inherent in us. It is what we have come from and what we will return to. It is within the middle part of that journey, from coming to going, that the unconditional part of love gets lost and found.

Conditional love hurts us and Unconditional love heals us.

It takes a courageous heart to travel from denial to self-awareness and then all the way to complete self-responsibility, for the temptation to stop along the way is strong within the ego.

We are spiritual beings having a physical, human experience, this has been said many times.

What is important about this is that our spiritual being does not negate our physical, humanness and our physical humanness does not invalidate our spiritual being.

We know that nothing anyone else ever does is about us and yet we want to make what they do the reason why we are hurting.

There is divine plan, created in the heart of the mother herself and lovingly bestowed upon all of her children that inhabit the earth.

We are her beloved, she is living her purpose for us, through us. Every life is sacred, every living thing is loved and cherished by the mother.

With love and gratitude, surrender yourself to this divine plan and allow the magic of life to unfold before you.

Forgiveness allows you to change your karmic consequence as you have to journey though self-awareness, understanding, empathy and compassion to arrive at it.

It takes surrender to forgive yourself and others, and acceptance that all people make mistakes and behave in ways that require forgiveness.

We are all working through our karmic consequences and creating them at the same time, learning through the contrast of duality and evolving into the heart centered wisdom of true being.

I will bury my self in the earth

Returning home the broken pieces of myself

Planting the dying fragments deep under the rich soil of Mother Earth herself

Where she will heal me and bring me back to life

The most noble pursuit is that of self-awareness for it is only through being self-aware that we can reach our most aligned state of being.

In seeing all of ourselves, in examining and being in relationship with all of who we are, we gain the understanding of how to be authentic, of how to align to our highest morality in thought, feeling and action to fully embody our most purest potential.

To become a vessel of unconditional love and bridge the gap between Ego and the Divine self so that the Ego becomes a conduit for the divine rather than for its own self-interest.

Your divinity is in your humanity. Not in just being a human but in the benevolence of your human nature.

To know your divinity, you must come to know the fullness of yourself; and when you do, when you arrive at that knowing, the truth of you will bring your heart into the holy union of self actualisation and your highest potential fulfilled.

The denial of your true worthiness is the ultimate trick of the Ego to facilitate its own longevity.

Every moment we experience in our lives was created by our past self. By the beliefs we held, the behaviours we demonstrated and the decisions we made. That is the experience of Karma. Tomorrow's manifestation from today's reality. No one is immune to this. Our karma is our own. We are not living in someone else's karmic consequence, impacted by their past. We are living in our own. It is not possible for someone else's karmic reality to impact on us unless that impact is the manifestation of our own karmic consequence, the impact from our past held beliefs, demonstrated behaviours and historical decisions.

Understanding this is a pathway to compassion, understanding and forgiveness for self and others. It is the journey back to love.

Change your future Karma by examining, owning and changing your now.

Truth is simply a perception and perception is merely interpretation.

Examine someone's interpretation and you will find there is more to the 'truth' than they can see.

Interpretation relies on previous experience, and previous experience can create unfavourable projection.

The unexamined truth is but a half truth.

Most of us have at times made the mistake of basing our belief on half-truths to our own detriment and perhaps the detriment of others. For action taken on half-truths has the power to condemn rather than liberate.

A moment will come when we stop hating, stop judging and learn to acknowledge our own and each others divine duality.

We are all alike in both shadow and light, and express both aspects of this duality, consciously and unconsciously.

Through learning this wisdom, we find unconditional love, peace and unity.

To choose to act out of love, to make our thoughts and deeds reflect the purity of love is our ultimate purpose.

To move aside the judgements and fear that stand in the way of our pure expression of love is the very pathway to enlightenment.

Love is our home, it is our natural state.

Love both wounds us and heals us, it both destroys us and offers us salvation and through that duality, it grows us.

Love expands our consciousness and demands us to find the courage to act with compassion in the face of our own outrage.

It asks us to move aside our pain enough to recognise the pain in another, to see that which makes us the same, to have understanding and to find the strength to offer mercy through the loving act of forgiveness.

Love asks us to share it, to offer what we have unconditionally to the world, to pass it on.

Love offers profound wisdom and guidance that leads to peace and grace, a heaven right here on earth, born of our own purified perception and sincere acts of service.

Love asks more of us, it asks us to let go of what we think we need in order to be ok, and tells us what we should give in order to be at peace.

Suffering is from the ego.

Suffer as long as you must but make sure you use it for your growth.

This chapter is not your whole story, the moment not your whole life.

This ending is only the beginning and your story is still being written.

Trust your life enough to embrace the art of living it.

No true Kingdom/Queendom was ever built by a heart too fearful to be pure.

We are changing.

Faster than ever before.

Can you feel it?

Think back over your life.

How different do you feel from the beginning of this year, from the beginning of this decade?

How many lives have you lived in this life so far?

How many versions of you have come and gone?

Each time your perspective of life, of yourself shifts, the universe that you existed in comes to an end and a whole new one begins.

If you were to come to understand this on the deepest level, you would fear no change, not even death itself, for there is no real death only a change of perspective.

Some changes are so subtle they go unnoticed and some are so radical they usher in a whole new experience of consciousness itself.

Surrender to the flow.

Let everything you think you know go.

Let change deliver you to where you soul awaits, calling you home.

It is time.

Love in its truest sense is not an emotion, it is a state of being, our true state of being, all of us.

Come back to who you really are. Come back to love.

Only through humility can you be honest with yourself and others.

This allows the death of the ego identity and the birth of true authenticity.

Humility is only achieved by fully letting go of any external perception and coming back to the truth that connects us all.

The place where we are all the same and the knowing that we are all traveling through this human experience, expressing light and dark, on the path to enlightenment.

To be humble is to be wholeheartedly living in truth.

Surrender and find peace in your heart, you can trust your life to unfold exactly as it should.

Have patience but most importantly pay attention!

A higher self is guiding you on this journey, feel into the depth of your being and there you will find your way.

Confusion about things that once made sense is a sign that you are elevating to a higher level of consciousness.

Awakening causes the collision of old and new paradigms and that results in time frames of confusion.

Find space to meditate and allow yourself to integrate your new awareness, this will help to clear the confusion.

Only once you Know Thyself, can you truly Be Thyself and that is what this life is calling for.

It is asking us to come into a state of Embodiment. Not of a certain teaching, or practice but of the very essence of our own true and unique soul nature.

To do the work to be become so self aware, that all there is left to do, is simply to be.

Only from this state, can we live a life of service to our highest most powerful potential. The potential that we came here to share with the world as a purpose, a devotion, an offering of truth and love.

You are the canvas, the paint and the painter.

Create your image however you choose, as all imagery is imaginary and artificial.

Life. You. My Mirror.

I feel your calling in my bones

Your whispers of truth in my heart

Singing my wildness home

Drawing out my hidden parts

Consciousness is always streaming through us, pulling us forward to the next moment, along the continuum of expansion.

Seemingly unrelated moments only reveal their secret synergistic nature when our expansion reaches a certain vantage point of recognition.

Cause and effect are always at play, weaving the tapestry of our reality.

Only once we stop being someone in order to belong to a few, then we are free to be with everything in unity.

We have to walk the path of the ego and be initiated by our own shadow before we earn the right to walk the path of our soul and fully embody our light.

It is our own Hero's Journey. Our own individual, tailor made story line of challenge, suffering, overcoming and liberation.

There will come a point where you see the story line so clearly, the set of challenges that you have struggled with over and over again in countless different scenarios. The places may have changed, the people, even the length of time each one plays out and yet you will see that you have always only ever had at the core of all of your melodrama, just a few unsupportive self beliefs that you have been up against and underneath those beliefs is the thing you fear the most. The cave you fear to enter but this cave holds your liberation you see!

The moment you chose to let go of trying to overcome the unsupportive beliefs that are just there to distract you from what is under them and face that fear, you begin the path of liberation. This my friend is the End Game. The moment you are passing from Ego to Soul, from Mind to Heart, from dreaming to awake, from the matrix to truth.

That is the journey you came here for. The only journey you will ever be on.

The journey to liberate your highest soul potential here in human form.

We are all on the same journey, each and every one of us. So have patience, have compassion, have understanding. This journey is hard, it is long and it has been mapped out for us before we got here. Knowing the difference between the I and the i will save you much suffering. You are the architect of this journey (the big I) and at the same time the experience of it (the little i).

So have faith, trust in yourself, you were made for this journey. Wherever you find yourself in your journey my friend, I see you, I see all of you, you are glorious and you've got this.

Not everyone will like you

Not everyone will treat you right

Not everyone will care about you

Not everyone will change their behaviour

Not everyone will be honest with you

Not everyone will see the best in you

Not everyone will love you

Not everyone will accept you as you are

Not everyone will have your best interest at heart

Not everyone will show up when you need them to

Not everyone will support your hopes and dreams

Not everyone will believe in you

Not everyone will say sorry when they should

Not everyone will be kind

Not everyone will try to understand you

Not everyone will have compassion for your mistakes

Not everyone will forgive you

And with all of that the two most important things for you are:

1. That you learn to accept this so it doesn't control you
2. That you are not one of those people to yourself

Sometimes to truly live you have to experience death.

You have to live out the death of your old life, your old self.

You have to live through the process of dying

The painful, aching, tormenting journey moment by moment.

Allowing yourself to succumb to it, as long as it takes in order to be re-birthed.

You cannot be open to love with a closed off heart.

Heal, release, let go, forgive, awaken. Do whatever you need to do, just open your heart.

Homecoming, is the greatest feeling in the world.

You will never experience love, peace or bliss as completely as when you return to your true self.

Returning to your true essence of divinity.

Conquering our deepest fear is like going Supernova.

We start with the contraction, imploding in on ourselves as our thoughts and vibration become more condensed.

There is less and less space with us, the deeper we go into the fear.

The density builds and builds as our whole world falls in on itself, right into the core of the fear as the gravity of it pulling us in wins out over our resistance to facing it.

At the moment of maximum density, where we are fully compressed is the very same moment we explode outwards, shattering and annihilating the fear itself.

That is the moment of liberation, where we burst open and our light pours out, brighter than ever before.

We become free and expansive and all that is left of the fear are the beautiful remnants of its existence that changed us forever and that in the end, set us free.

Where there is fear, there is courage recognising itself.

Every spiritual message ever shared is layered in dimensional perspective because our experience of reality is governed by dimensional perspective.

The dimensions are measured by different degrees of vibrational frequency. From the lower and slower frequencies to the higher and faster frequencies.

The layering of perception creates different vantage points from which to view reality from. Many dimensions of understanding are shared at once in order to allow the reader to resonate with the message at their current level of dimensional perceiving.

The more we expand through the opening of our third eye/pineal gland, the more dimensions we begin to perceive from and so our experience of reality expands into more and more layers of awareness and so becomes multidimensional.

This is the process of Awakening, the expanding through dimensional perspectives until the ultimate awakening from all perspectives back into the singularity in which all dimensions came from in the beginning.

As in the beginning, so it is in the end.

Lovingly witness the Ego but don't feed it.

If you are seeing it, then you know that you are not it.

Give it love but not life.

Love is the only way.

i

What you experience through others is the unintegrated parts of self. There is no outside, it is just the reflection of the inside.

Like when you look into a mirror, there are not two people, just you and your external experience of you through the reflection in the mirror.

If you want to see the reflection smile, who has to smile?

The journey from suffering to liberation is a continuum of the recognition of resistance to healing and the subsequent releasing of it.

The moment that all of our resistance has been released, is the moment that we will be healed and therefore liberated.

If we do no realize and release our resistance to the healing journey, we will stop along the way and instead empower ourselves as victims.

An empowered victim is someone who has not mastered the healing journey and liberated themselves into their divine sovereign power. They stay stuck in the experiences that traumatised them and only empower their pain which keeps them in the experience and being constantly reoffended. They have to empower themselves within their trauma because they are not yet willing to truly heal and come to completion with it.

We have the strength to heal from what we have endured if we can find the courage to walk the path of liberation.

Our pain is real and valid but so is the possibility of liberation and ultimately it is our free will choice as to whether or not we become an Empowered Victim living or Empowered Victor.

With deep courage, compassion and understanding we can walk the path that sets us free, the path of self mastery.

Everything happens when it is time.

Not a moment before or a moment after but in the perfect moment for it to happen.

Life is a tapestry, beautifully woven and intricately designed.

The more you soften into the mystery, the more you allow it to take you where you are going, the more joyful your experience is.

You are not really in control of where you are heading in each moment, not in the way that you think you are. There are subtitles of creation and manifestation that are beyond the EGO construct.

The universe, consciousness is not capitalistic, it doesn't manifest things for the sake of having things, it manifests experience for the sake of expansion.

When things come into your experience, they are there because they will facilitate the experience that consciousness is manifesting through you.

When you cultivate faith, you let go and allow the experience that is trying to be had to come fully into your awareness. It is always there in full, you are just not always aware of the whole and as such often focus on only a portion of the fullness of the moment that is available to you.

This make life seem unfair or unjust when the full picture of beneficial expansion can not be seen and acknowledged and therefore not experienced.

You get to decide how much of the full experience you have. You get to decide how open you are to it all, moment by moment.

That is your free will, your sovereign right and your responsibility.

You are not intimidated by what you think people are but by what you think you are not.

The Ego death doesn't happen in one go. It is a process of dying over and over again.

Like a snake sheds its skin when it out grows it, we too shed the layers of our outer Ego construct as we out grow them.

Each shedding is a death and is the ending of a universe of perspective.

Your own multiverse within your layers of perception.

It is an automatic process, the more present you become with yourself the more you recognise the subtle shifts as your experience of reality changes. You become aware of the dynamic nature of your perception of life itself and learn to live within the fluidness of the constant cycle of death and rebirth.

You are sacred geometry, fractal in nature, ever morphing with infinite iterations.

You recognise all of the world as you once you have fully realised your self as ONE.

Until you are the embodiment of oneness, you see yourself in the mirrors of reflection made visible to you through the experience of others.

Once fully realised the mirrors fall away and all is transparent and obvious in its divinity.

The Divine One masquerading as other than itself until each mask is realised and released and all is revealed to all so that all can know itself as one.

Ascension is the embodying of yourself as the Divine One in thought, word and action within all of your incarnations happening simultaneously in all dimensions of time and space.

Go deep into yourself

Deeper than ever before

All the way to the place where you split yourself in two

The core of duality that resides within

Deep in your subconscious self

Where you split light and dark from one into two, remember

You made this choice

You ask to know them as different sides of the one experience

It was always you

Choosing to know yourself in every way possible, remember

They were never separate, light and dark are one not two, remember

It was always you, casting shadows in the light to know them as two, remember now

YOU

ARE

ONE

NOT

TWO

Wake up

Remember

You are more than this

You are here for a reason

Your life is calling you

Open to the truth

Live through love

You know what to do

Listen

Follow the calling

Trust

Have faith

Rise

Speak

There is no other time but NOW

Are you remembering now?

Do you feel the dawn arriving on your next breath?

Awakening is but a moment away in the infinite now.

You are so close to being you, so very nearly yourself that you are beginning to recognise who you are.

The reflections are falling, everything is becoming transparent and true in its own nature.

You can hear the calling of grace, singing you home. Moving you along and stretching you out through the vibration of its angelic tone.

You are but one moment, one awareness, one recognition away from crossing the bridge along The Way to embodying your sacred truth and stepping into the Holy Halls of your own crowned sovereignty.

The moment you allow that thought, open to that awareness and accept that recognition, your initiation is done and you will birth yourself upon your own humble throne.

Our emotions are not enemies that need to be forced into submission.

Rather they are fragile children who need to feel safe and be acknowledged.

Everything is ONE, so Unity is the only reality.

Temple of the Sacred Light

Wherever you go, there is a Temple for the Temple is within.

You are a sacred and holy vessel, a portal for the light of all that is to shine through.

A fractal of consciousness on a journey of remembering its wholeness.

Look within, become aware of your awareness, be conscious of your consciousness and you will commune with the light of your soul, the truth of your essence, the I Am that I Am that you are.

Go inwards to your Temple every day and honor the sacredness of the light with absolute devotion and you will align yourself to the purity of truth.

Open your heart and bow down in holy reverence to the light as manifest in all forms and you will align yourself with the grace and mercy of love.

Look through your third eye and you will see through the veil of perception and the illusion of the Maya will fall before you to reveal the glory of the eternal perfection.

About the Author:

With over 10 years of experience as a Master Coach and Mentor and over 6 years experience of writing and delivering deeply healing Workshops & Retreats, Ra has an in-depth understanding of human psychology and how to support people to come into higher levels of awareness and consciousness.

Ra is a seeker - and Mentor. Pursuing in her life greater and greater.. - awareness, through her own personal journey.

Passionately sharing over a decade of experience with breath work, guided meditation, psychotherapy, experiential process work, shadow work, facilitation, content creation. guided rituals, leadership mentoring and personal mentoring and training new coaches. Ra supports new coaches in this field through her Transformational Coach Training Program.

Ra has co-facilitated and shared her own powerful events all over Australia.

Self awareness, self acceptance, self responsibility, self love, self expression. Ultimately, liberation is why she lives.

With a mix of understanding, experience, compassion and a deep deep love for all people, Ra holds a space of inclusivity, non judgement and absolute permission for you to show up as you are and discover your pure authenticity and the truth of your divine essence.

www.ingramcontent.com/pod-product-compliance
Lightning Source LLC
Chambersburg PA
CBHW050313010526
44107CB00055B/2222